W9-DHJ-283

Hamlet

Hamlet

Illustrated by Cal Williams

MACMILLAN • USA

MACMILLAN
A Simon & Schuster Macmillan Company
1633 Broadway
New York, NY 10019

First published in 1996 by
Appletree Press Ltd,
19-21 Alfred Street,
Belfast BT2 8DL.

MACMILLAN is a trademark of Macmillan, Inc.
Library of Congress Cataloging-in-Publication Data
Shakespeare, William, 1564-1616.
  Hamlet: shorter Shakespeare/William Shakespeare.
    p. cm.
  ISBN 0-02-861232-9
1. Shakespeare, William, 1564-1616–Adaptations. I. Title.
PR2878.H3 1996
822.3'3–dc20   96-16135
                                                    CIP

Printed in Singapore

10 9 8 7 6 5 4 3 2 1

Hamlet might well claim to be Shakespeare's most famous play because of its language and the fascination of its protagonist. The persistent appeal of the character and the sense of the confined world of Elsinore - "Denmark's a prison" - have tempted many actors and directors to read the play as a psychological drama.

The Denmark of the play is an elective kingdom with no automatic right of succession. Hamlet may be the eldest son of the late king, but he is not the heir to the throne. This is highly significant since it aggravates Hamlet's situation and helps explain the importance of Polonius's position. Polonius may appear to be a garrulous, self-important bore, but he is clearly a master of politics. When Claudius, Hamlet's uncle, was vying for the crown, it was Polonius's lobbying of the members of the electoral college (nobles and senior religious) that secured Claudius the throne. Likewise, the art of diplomacy is one in which Claudius is well versed, as is evidenced by his dealings with ambassadors. Gertrude, the queen, is not native to Denmark as her cry 'False Danish dogs' makes clear, and no doubt she formed a significant part of some earlier diplomatic pact or treaty.

The play was first performed in 1600 and, though no period for the play's action is indicated, it would appear to draw heavily on events that happened during the late sixteenth century. The clash of Protestant and Catholic theology in the Reformation is definitely an influence on the play. Hamlet and his friend, Horatio, are clearly influenced by Reformation ideas, their school of thought being that of Martin Luther. Hamlet's debates about immortality shows him to be on the side of the Puritans. Yet his acceptance of such Catholic beliefs as purgatory and the capacity that the devil has "to assume a pleasing shape" shows that the older religion still has a grip.

The great richness of the play and the reasons for its continuing international popularity can be found in all of these elements. Hamlet, torn between feelings of revenge and the kinder spirit of the humanist Renaissance, is a modern Everyman who speaks to everyone whom conscience makes a coward of.

> *Hamlet, Prince of Denmark, was first performed in 1600.*

Hamlet

It is after midnight on the battlements of Elsinore
Castle, Denmark. Barnardo and Marcellus, the officers
of the watch, have a companion with them - Horatio,
a fellow student of Prince Hamlet, the son of the late
King. Horatio is sceptical about their story that they have
twice seen the ghost of the dead king, but has agreed to
join them on the upper battlements to see for himself.

MARCELLUS: Look where it comes again.

BARNARDO: In the same figure like the King, that's dead.

MARCELLUS: Thou art a scholar, speak to it, Horatio.

BARNARDO: Looks it not like the king? Mark it, Horatio.

HORATIO: Most like. It harrows me with fear and wonder.

BARNARDO: It would be spoke to.

MARCELLUS: Question it, Horatio.

HORATIO: What art thou that usurps't this time of night,
　　Together with that fair and warlike form
　　In which the majesty of buried Denmark
　　Did sometimes march? By Heaven, I charge thee
　　　　speak.

MARCELLUS: It is offended.

BARNARDO: See! It stalks away.

　　The ghost leaves and the three cover their unease by chatting about politics and the preparations for possible war against Fortinbras, the young nephew of the ageing king of Norway. This is interrupted by the return of the ghost. The spirit finally fades when the cock crows morning. Horatio is eager to tell Hamlet the news and is sure that the king's ghost will speak to his son.

HORATIO: Break we our watch up, and by my advice.
　　Let us impart what we have seen tonight
　　Unto young Hamlet; for upon my life

This spirit dumb to us will speak to him.

In the great hall of the castle, Claudius, the king, is holding a solemn council. Claudius is the younger brother of the late king, who died after being bitten by a serpent. Polonius, Claudius's counsellor stands close to the king and his queen, Gertrude, the widow of the late king and mother of Hamlet. The king addresses Hamlet, whose grief at his beloved father's death and dismay at his mother's hasty marriage to his uncle seem to have unhinged him.

KING: But now, my cousin Hamlet, and my son.

HAMLET: (*Aside*) A little more than kin, and less than kind...

KING: 'Tis sweet and commendable in your nature,
        Hamlet,
     To give these mourning duties to your father...
     We pray you throw to earth
     This unprevailing woe, and think of us
     As of a father; for let the world take note
     You are the most immediate to our throne...
     And we beseech you, bend you to remain
     Here in the cheer and comfort of our eye,
     Our chiefest courtier, cousin and our son.

The council ends and Hamlet is left alone. He wishes

that he could kill himself, but knows this to be against God's will. He remembers how his father had loved Gertrude.

HAMLET: O that this too too solid flesh would melt,
　　Thaw and resolve itself into a dew,
　　Or that the Everlasting had not fixed
　　His canon 'gainst self-slaughter. O God! God!
　　How weary, stale, flat and unprofitable
　　Seem to me all the uses of this world!
　　But two months dead nay, nor so much, not two:
　　So excellent a king... so loving to my mother
　　That he might not beteem the winds of heaven
　　Visit her face too roughly.

As Hamlet dwells on his mother's marriage to her brother-in-law less than two months after her husband's death, it makes him doubt all women in general.

HAMLET: Let me not think on it: frailty thy name is woman
　　O God! A beast that wants discourse of reason,
　　Would have mourned longer

His bitter thoughts are interrupted by the entrance of Horatio and Marcellus. Hamlet greets Horatio warmly and asks what brings him to Elsinore.

HAMLET: But what is your affair in Elsinore?

We'll teach you to drink deep ere you depart.

HORATIO: My lord, I came to see your father's funeral.

HAMLET: I prithee, do not mock me, fellow-student.
I think it was to see my mother's wedding.

HORATIO: Indeed, my lord, it follow'd hard upon.

HAMLET: Thrift, Horatio, thrift. The funeral baked meats
Did coldly furnish forth the marriage tables.

Horatio then tells Hamlet about the ghost and answers all of the prince's anxious questions. Hamlet warns his friends to say nothing, and arranges to meet them that night on the battlements. When they leave, Hamlet paces about the empty hall, fearful yet excited.

HAMLET: My father's spirit in arms! All is not well.
I doubt some foul play. Would the night were come.
Till then sit still, my soul. Foul deeds will rise
Though all the earth overwhelm them, to men's eyes.

Meanwhile Laertes, Polonius's son, prepares to leave for France. His father gives him some advice.

POLONIUS: Give thy thoughts no tongue
Nor any unproportioned thought his act.
Be thou familiar but by no means vulgar;
Those friends thou hast and their adoption tried,
Grapple them to thy soul like hoops of steel...
Give every man thy ear, but few thy voice;
Take each man's censure, but reserve thy judgement...
Neither a borrower nor a lender be,
For loan oft loses both itself and friend
And borrowing dulls the edge of husbandry.
This above all: to thine own self be true,
And it must follow as the night the day
Thou canst not then be false to any man.

As Laertes kisses his sister, Ophelia, goodbye he says "Remember well what I have said to you." After Laertes leaves, Polonius questions Ophelia as to what Laertes meant.

OPHELIA: So please you, something touching the Lord
        Hamlet...
He hath, my lord, of late made many tenders
Of his affection to me.

Polonius grows very angry and warns Ophelia not

to see Hamlet.

POLONIUS: I would not, in plain terms, from this time
forth
Have you so slander any moments leisure
As to give words or talk with the Lord Hamlet.
Look to it, I charge you.

That night, Hamlet, Horatio, and Marcellus wait expectantly on the battlements. They can hear sounds of revelry in Claudius's court and as Hamlet voices his disapproval, he is interrupted by the entrance of the ghost. Hamlet is shocked but speaks to the spirit.

HAMLET: Angels and ministers of grace defend us!
Be thou a spirit of health or goblin damned,
Bring with thee airs from heaven or blasts from hell,

Be thy intents wicked or charitable,
Thou comest in such a questionable shape
That I will speak to thee. I call thee Hamlet,
King, father, royal Dane.

MARCELLUS: Look with what courteous action
It waves you to a more removed ground:
But do not go with it.

HORATIO: No, by no means.

HAMLET : It will not speak; then I will follow it.

HORATIO: Do not my lord.

Despite his companions' attempts to restrain him, Hamlet insists on following the apparition. Eventually, when they are quite alone, the spirit speaks for the first time. It is his father's spirit, who cannot rest until his murder has been revenged.

GHOST: Revenge his foul and most unnatural murder.

HAMLET: Murder!

GHOST: Murder most foul, as in the best it is,
But this most strange, foul and unnatural.

HAMLET: Haste me to know it that I with wings as swift

As meditation, or the thoughts of love,
May sweep to my revenge.

GHOST: 'Tis given out that, sleeping in my orchard,
 A serpent stung me; so the whole ear of Denmark
 Is by a forged process of my death
 Rankly abused; but know, thou noble youth,
 The serpent that did sting thy father's life
 Now wears his crown.

HAMLET: O my prophetic soul, my uncle!

Having accused Claudius of his murder, the ghost explains the circumstances of his death. The king was sleeping when his brother poured a deadly poison into his ears.

GHOST: Brief let me be. Sleeping in my orchard,
 My custom always of the afternoon,
 Upon my secure hour thy uncle stole
 With juice of cursed hebenon in a vial,
 And in the porches of my ears did pour

The leprous distilment, whose effect
Holds such an enmity with blood of man
That swift as quicksilver it courses through
The natural gates and alleys of the body...
And a most instant tetter barked about
Most lazar-like, with a vile and loathsome crust
All my smooth body.
Thus was I, sleeping, by a brother's hand
Of life, of crown, of queen at once dispatched.

The spirit then fades as dawn breaks. Marcellus and
Horatio come running in, worried about Hamlet. He
makes them swear not to speak of what they have seen
and they oblige. They learn that Hamlet intends to cover
his real intent with the appearance of eccentricity or madness.

HAMLET: There are more things in heaven and earth
           Horatio,
   Than are dreamt of in your philosophy...
   I perchance hereafter shall think meet
   To put an antick dipsosition on.

During the following weeks, Hamlet's behavior causes
Claudius and Gertrude a great deal of worry. But
Polonius assumes that it is thwarted love for Ophelia that
so troubles Hamlet.

POLONIUS: ... I precepts gave her,
   That she should lock herself from his resort,
   Admit no messengers, receive no tokens.
   Which done, she took the fruits of my advice;
   And he, repulsed - a short tale to make -
   Fell into a sadness; then into a fast;
   Thence to a watch; thence into weakness;
   Thence into a lightness; and, by this declension,
   Into the madness wherein now he raves -
   And all we wail for.

As a means of spying on Hamlet, Claudius sends for Rosencrantz and Guildenstern, two of Hamlet's school-friends. Hamlet explains his melancholy to them but not the reason for it.

HAMLET: I have of late and wherefore I know not, lost all my mirth, foregone all custom of exercises; and indeed it goes so heavily with my disposition that this goodly frame, the earth seems to me a sterile promontory, this most excellent canopy the air, look you, this brave o'er-hanging firmament, this majestical roof fretted with golden fire, why, it appeareth nothing to me but a foul and pestilent congregation of vapours. What a piece of work is a man, how noble and reason, how infinite in faculties, in form and moving how express and admirable, in action how like an angel, in apprehension how like a god: the beauty of the world, the paragon of animals. And yet to me what is this quintessence of dust? Man delights not me nor woman neither, though by your smiling you seem to say so.

Hamlet cheers up with the arrival of a troupe of travelling players and arranges that they should perform a popular play, *The Mousetrap*, into which he will insert a "speech of some dozen or sixteen lines." Hamlet intends to have the players re-enact the murder of King Hamlet to gauge Claudius's guilt for himself.

HAMLET: I'll have these players
  Play something like the murder of my father
  Before mine uncle. I'll observe his looks:
  I'll tent him to the quick. If he but blench
  I know my course. The spirit I have seen
  May be the devil, and the devil has power
  T'assume a pleasing shape, yea, and perhaps,
  Out of my weakness and my melancholy,
  As he is very potent with such spirits,
  Abuses me to damn me. I'll have grounds
  More relative than this. The play's the thing
  Wherein I'll catch the conscience of the King.

Rosencrantz and Guildenstern are questioned by Gertrude and Claudius about Hamlet's condition but can only say that he seems interested in the play that the travelling company is to present that night.

Polonius then persuades the king to eavesdrop at an "accidental" meeting which Polonius will arrange

between Hamlet and Ophelia. Unaware of the onlookers, Hamlet enters debating whether it is better to live or die.

HAMLET: To be, or not to be, that is the question
  Whether it is nobler in the mind to suffer
  The slings and arrows of outrageous fortune,
  Or to take arms against a sea of troubles
  And by opposing end them. To die to sleep,
  No more; and by a sleep to say we end
  The heartaches and the thousand natural shocks
  That flesh is heir to: 'tis a consummation

Devoutly to be wished. To die, to sleep;
To sleep, perchance to dream: ay there's the rub:
For in that sleep of death what dreams may come,
When we have shuffled off this mortal coil,
Must give us pause. There's the respect
That makes calamity of so long life.
For who would bear the whips and scorns of time,
Th'oppressors' wrong, the proud man's contumely,
The pangs of despised love, the law's delay,
The insolence of office, and the spurns
That patient merit of the unworthy takes
When he himself might his quietus make
With a bare bodkin? Who would fardels bear,
To grunt and sweat under a weary life,
But that the dread of something after death,
The undiscovered country from whose bourn
No traveller returns, puzzles the will,
And makes us rather bear those ills we have
Than fly to others that we know not of?
Thus conscience does make cowards of us all,
And thus the native hue of resolution
Is sicklied over with the pale cast of thought,
And enterprises of great pith and moment
With this regard their currents turn awry
And lose the name of action. Soft you now,
The fair Ophelia! Nymph, in thy orisons
Be all my sins remembered.

OPHELIA: Good my lord,
How does your honour for this many a day?

HAMLET: I humbly thank you, well.

OPHELIA: My lord, I have remembrances of yours
That I have longed long to be redeliver.
I pray you now receive them.

Hamlet denies sending anything to Ophelia and there is then a scene of bitter recrimination in which Hamlet launches into a stinging attack on womankind.

HAMLET: I never gave you aught.

OPHELIA: My honour'd lord, you know right well you did;
And, with them, words of so sweet breath compos'd
As made the things more rich: their perfume lost,
Take these again; for, to the noble mind,
Rich gifts wax poor when givers prove unkind.
There my lord.

HAMLET: I did love you once.

OPHELIA: Indeed, my lord, you made me believe so.

HAMLET: You should not have believed me; for virtue cannot so inoculate our old stock, but we shall relish of it. I loved you not.

OPHELIA: I was the more deceived.

HAMLET: If thou dost marry, I'll give thee this plague for thy dowry. Be thou as chaste as ice, as pure as snow, thou shalt not escape calumny. Get thee to a nunnery; go, farewell. Or if thou wilt needs marry, marry a fool for wise men know well enough what monsters you make of them. To a nunnery, go; and quickly too. Farewell.

When Hamlet and Ophelia leave, Claudius and Polonius discuss what they have seen and heard. Although Claudius does not understand exactly what is wrong with Hamlet, he discerns that there is danger in the offing, and so resolves to send Hamlet to England.

KING: Love, his affections did not that way tend,
    Nor what he spake, though it lacked form a little,
    Was not like madness. There's something in his soul
    O'er which his melancholy sits on brood,

And I do doubt the hatch and the disclose
Will be some danger; which for to prevent,
I have with quick determination
Thus set it down: he shall with speed to England
For the demand of our neglected tribute.

Polonius asks the king to wait until after the play, to give Gerturde a chance to speak to her son, and try to find out what is troubling him. Polonius also tells the king that he will hide and report back what happens.

KING: It shall be so.
Madness in great ones must not unwatched go.

Before the play begins, Hamlet explains to Horatio that he will watch Claudius's reaction closely to assess his guilt. The whole court attends the play, given in the council chamber. When Claudius hears the opening lines he grows restless, but when he sees the player king being lulled to sleep by the player queen, and the nephew, Lucianus, pour poison in the king's ear, he rises from his throne shouting.

OPHELIA: The King rises.

HAMLET: What, frighted with false fire?

QUEEN: How fares my lord?

POLONIUS: Give over the play.

KING: Give me some lights. Away.

The hall empties quickly and Hamlet and Horatio are left alone. Hamlet turns excitedly to his friend:

HAMLET: O good Horatio! I'll take the ghost's word for a thousand pounds. Did'st perceive?

HORATIO: Very well, my lord.

The king orders Rosencrantz and Guildenstern to discover Hamlet's mood and take him a summons from his mother. The king has already made arrangements for Hamlet to carry letters to England and have him killed. Rosencrantz and Guildenstern are to accompany the prince to make sure the deed is done. Polonius enters as Rosencrantz and Guildenstern leave, and tells the king that he is on his way to eavesdrop on Hamlet's conversation with his mother.

POLONIUS: It is meet that some more audience than a mother,
Since nature makes them partial, should overhear
The speech, of vantage.

When Polonius leaves, the king is left on his own and, unnerved by the play, has an attack of conscience. He

admits that he has killed his brother and asks God for pardon. Yet he acknowledges that to be properly pardoned he should give up all he has gained as a result of that foul murder - his crown, his queen, and his ambition. Nevertheless, he sinks to his kneels and prays. Hamlet passes by as Claudius is praying. Seeing his enemy, alone and unprotected, Hamlet is tempted to kill him immediately.

HAMLET: Now might I do it pat, now he is a-praying.
    And now I'll do it.

He draws his sword and holds it above Claudius's neck, ready to strike. Then he pauses. He changes his mind, thinking that it is inappropriate to kill a praying man. He will wait until Claudius is asleep, drunk or angry.

HAMLET: Why, this is hire and salary, not revenge...
Up sword, and know thou a more horrid hent:
When he is drunk asleep, or in his rage,
Or in th'incestuous pleasure of his bed...
Then trip him up, that his heels may kick at heaven
And that his soul may be as damn'd and black
As hell, whereto it goes.

Hamlet sheaths his sword and goes to his mother's bedroom. Polonius hears Hamlet's footsteps and hides behind a tapestry. When Hamlet enters he is still angry and crudely insults his mother.

HAMLET: Now, mother, what's the matter?

QUEEN: Hamlet, thou has thy father much offended.

HAMLET: Mother, you have my father much offended.

QUEEN: Come, come, you answer with an idle tongue.

HAMLET: Go, go, you question with a wicked tongue.

As tempers flare, Gertrude is about to call the guards, when Hamlet pushes her down.

HAMLET: You go not till I set you up a glass
Where you may see the inmost part of you.

QUEEN: What wilt thou do? Thou wilt not murder me?

Gertrude screams for help and Polonius, from his hiding place, echoes her cries. Hamlet thrusts his sword through the tapestry into the concealed figure. When he pulls aside the drape he finds himself faced with the corpse of Polonius, and not the king as he had expected.

QUEEN: O what a rash and bloody deed is this?

HAMLET: A bloody deed. Almost as bad, good mother,
As kill a king and marry with his brother.

QUEEN: As kill a king?

HAMLET: Aye, lady it was my word
Thou wretched rash intruding fool, farewell.
I took thee for thy better.

Hamlet's charges his mother with her "adultery" and the scandalous speed of her marriage and compares her new husband, Claudius, to Hamlet's father, the late king.

QUEEN: What have I done, that thou darest wag thy
tongue
In noise so rude against me?

HAMLET: Such an act,
That blurs the grace and blush of modesty;

Calls virtue, hypocrite; takes off the rose
From the fair forehead of an innocent love,
And sets a blister there; makes marriage vows
As false as dicers' oaths: O! such a deed,
As from the body of contraction plucks
The very soul; and sweet religion makes
A rhapsody of words: heaven's face doth glow;
Yea, this solidity and compound mass.
With tristful visage, as against the doom,
Is thought-sick at the act.

QUEEN: Ah me! what act,
That roars so loud, and thunders in the index?

HAMLET. Look here, upon this picture, and on this;
The counterfeit presentment of two brothers.
See, what a grace was seated on this brow:
Hyperion's curls: the front of Jove himself;
An eye like Mars, to threaten and command;
A station like the herald Mercury,
New lighted on a heaven-kissing hill;
A combination, and a form, indeed,
Where every god did seem to set his seal,
To give the world assurance of a man.
This was your husband: look you now, what follows.
Here is your husband; like mildew'd ear,
Blasting his wholesome brother. Have you eyes?

You cannot call it love; for, at your age,
The hey-day in the blood is tame, it's humble,
And waits upon the judgment; and what judgment
Would step from this to this?

He is interrupted by the entry of the Ghost, who is invisible to Gertrude. The queen takes Hamlet's conversation with the ghost as further proof of his madness.

QUEEN: Alas! how is't with you,
That you do bend your eye on vacancy,
And with the corporal air do hold discourse?
Forth at your eyes your spirits wildly peep;
And, as the sleeping soldiers in the alarm,
Your bedded hair, like life in excrements,
Starts up, and stands on end. O gentle son!

Upon the heat and flame of thy distemper
Sprinkle cool patience. Whereon do you look?

HAMLET: On him, on him!—Look you, how pale he glares!
His form and cause conjoin'd, preaching to stones,
Would make them capable.—Do not look upon me;
Lest with this piteous action you convert
My stern effects: then, what I have to do
Will want true colour; tears, perchance, for blood.

QUEEN: To whom do you speak this?

HAMLET: Why, look you there! look, how it steals away!
My father, in his habit as he liv'd!
Look, where he goes, even now, out at the portal!

QUEEN: This is the very coinage of your brain:
This bodiless creation ecstacy
Is very cunning in.

By the time Hamlet is ready to leave, dragging out
Polonius's body, Gertrude is shocked, tearful, and contrite
and Hamlet's mood has calmed.

HAMLET: Once more, good night
And when you are desirous to be blest,
I'll blessing beg of you.

Remorseful, Gertrude tells Claudius of the death of

Polonius. Hamlet will tell no one where the body is hidden, and it is not until he is marched to the throne room under armed guard that he finally answers the king's repeated question:

CLAUDIUS: Where is Polonius?

HAMLET: In heaven. Send thither to see. If your messenger find him not there, seek him in the other place yourself. But indeed if you find him not within this month, you shall nose him as you go up the stairs into the lobby.

Claudius, patient and well in control, tells Hamlet that "for thine especial safety" he will be sent to England. Hamlet can do little but comply. Meanwhile, Ophelia, distracted at her father's death, has lost her senses.

HORATIO: She speaks much of her father; says she hears
    There are tricks in the world; and hems and beats her
        heart;
    Spurns enviously at straws; speaks things in doubt,
    That carry but half sense; her speech is nothing ...

Shortly after hearing of his father's death, Laertes returns to Denmark and bursts into the royal apartments, shouting "Give me my father." Claudius soon calms Laertes but, just as he begins to explain what has happened, Ophelia enters the room. In her madness, she does not recognize her brother and Laertes is overwhelmed.

LAERTES: O heat, dry up my brains! Tears seven times salt,
Burn out the sense and virtue of mine eye!
By Heaven, thy madness shall be paid by weight
Till our scale turn the beam. O rose of May!
Dear maid, kind sister, sweet Ophelia!
O heavens! is it possible a young maid's wits
Should be as mortal as an old man's life?

OPHELIA: (*singing*) They bore him barefac'd on the bier;
Hey non nonny, nonny, hey nonny;
And in his grave rain'd many a tear ...

LAERTES: Hadst thou thy wits, and didst persuade
revenge
It could not move thus.

A few weeks later, some sailors arrive with letters from Hamlet for Horatio and the king and queen, informing them that, despite being attacked by pirates and taken prisoner, the prince will be returning shortly. When the

news reaches Laertes and Claudius, they begin to plot how Laertes will be revenged. Laertes will fence with Hamlet using an unprotected sword tipped with a deadly poison.

KING: He being remiss,
    Most generous, and free from all contriving,
    Will not peruse the foils; so that with ease,
    Or with a little shuffling, you may choose
    A sword unbated, and, in a pass of practice,
    Requite him for your father.

LAERTES: I'll anoint my sword ...
    With this contagion, that if I gall him slightly,
    It may be death.

The king then suggests that the wine at the match

should also be poisoned:

KING: And that he calls for drink, I'll have prepared him
    A chalice for the nonce, whereon but sipping,
    If he by any chance escape your venom'd stroke,
    Our purpose may hold there.

The Queen interrupts with the news that Ophelia has been drowned. A branch of the willow, on which Ophelia liked to sit weaving flower chains, broke, throwing the young maid into the brook.

QUEEN: ... an envious sliver broke,
    When down her weedy trophies and herself
    Fell in the weeping brook. Her clothes spread wide,
    And mermaid-like awhile they bore her up
    Which time she chanted snatches of old lauds,
    As one incapable of her own distress
    Or like a creature native and indued
    Unto that element. But long it could not be
    Till that her garments, heavy with their drink
    Pull'd the poor wretch from her melodious lay
    To muddy death.

Meanwhile, Hamlet has secretly arrived back in Denmark. He meets Horatio at the outskirts of Elsinore, and the pair are making their way to the castle when they hear a gravedigger, singing as he works. The gravedigger

shows Hamlet a skull which has been buried for twenty-three years; 'This same skull, sir, was Yorick's skull, the King's jester'. Hamlet takes the skull and is moved to speak.

HAMLET: Alas, poor Yorick. I knew him, Horatio, a fellow of infinite jest, most excellent fancy. He hath bore me on his back a thousand times, and now, how abhorred in my imagination it is. My gorge rises at it. Here hung those lips that I have kissed I know not how oft. Where be your jibes now, your gambols, your songs, your flashes of merriment, that were wont to set the table upon a roar? No one now to mock your own grinning? Quite chop-fallen? Now get you to my lady's chamber and tell her, let her paint an inch thick, to this favour she must come. Make her laugh at that.

He breaks off at the approach of a funeral. Seeing the court in attendance, he watches to see whose funeral it is. He overhears Laertes arguing with a priest, who questions Laertes's right to bury this possible suicide victim in sanctified ground.

PRIEST: She should in ground unsanctified been lodged
    Till the last trumpet: for charitable prayers
    Shards, flints, and pebbles should be thrown on her...

LAERTES: Lay her in the earth,

And from her fair and unpolluted flesh
May violets spring. I tell thee, churlish priest,
A ministering angel shall my sister be when thou
Liest howling.

Hamlet is shocked to hear the funeral is that of his lady
Ophelia. Then Laertes jumps into the grave and
clasps the body of Ophelia to him, calling to the gravedig-
gers to bury them both together. Hamlet comes out of hiding and also jumps into the grave, shouting.

HAMLET: What is he whose grief
  Bears such an emphasis, whose phrase of sorrow
  Conjures the wand'ring stars and makes them stand
  Like wonder-wounded hearers? This is I
  Hamlet the Dane.

LAERTES: The devil take thy soul!

A desperate struggle then ensues; Hamlet wrestling
with Laertes until they are separated by the guards.
Hamlet protests his love for Ophelia and asks why
Laertes has atacked him so.

HAMLET: I lov'd Ophelia. Forty thousand brothers
  Could not with their quantity of love
  Make up my sum...
  Hear you, sir,

What is the reason that you use me thus?

With that he climbs out of the grave and leaves the churchyard. The king sends Horatio after him and, turning to Laertes, whispers that their plan will soon be in effect.

KING: I pray you, good Horatio, wait upon him.
    (*To Laertes*) Strengthen your patience in our last night's
        speech;
    We'll put the matter to the present push.
    Good Gertrude, set some watch over your son.
    This grave shall have a living monument;
    An hour of quiet shortly shall we see;
    Till then, in patience our proceeding be.

Later, in the castle, Hamlet tells Horatio about his voyage

and shows him the orders from Claudius instructing that Hamlet be executed. However, Hamlet changed the order to read that the bearers of the message, Rosencrantz and Guildenstern, be put to death.

HAMLET: Ah, royal knavery! an exact command...
    That on the supervise, no leisure bated,
    No, not to stay the grinding of the axe,
    My head should be struck off.

HORATIO: Is it possible?

HAMLET: Here's the commission, read it with more leisure.
    But wilt thou hear now how I did proceed?

HORATIO: I beseech you.

HAMLET: ... I sat me down,
    Devised a new communication, wrote it fair...
    An earnest conjuration from the King,
    As England was his faithful tributary...
    He should those bearers put to sudden death,
    Not shriving-time allowed.

They are interrupted by Osric, a very dandified courtier, who delivers Laertes's challenge to the fencing match. Hamlet says that he will take part, but confides to Horatio that he feels strangely depressed. Horatio urges him to obey his instincts and withdraw from the match.

HAMLET: It is but foolery, but it is such a kind of gaingiving as would perhaps trouble a woman.

HORATIO: If your mind dislike anything, obey it. I will forestall their repair hither and say you are not fit.

Just before the first bout the king orders that cups of the tainted wine be set upon the table. The match begins and Hamlet proves clearly the superior fencer, winning the first two bouts. Gertrude proposes a toast to Hamlet's continued good fortune and unknowingly, drinks a glass of the poisoned wine. Laertes, enraged at his failure, stabs Hamlet with a foul blow, whereupon Hamlet resumes fighting and knocks Laertes's rapier from his hand, and as a result the pair swap swords. In the next bout, Hamlet wounds Laertes, but stops fighting when he sees his mother fall from her throne.

QUEEN: The drink, the drink! I'm poisoned.

HAMLET: Ho villainy! Ho! Let the door be lock'd
  Treachery! Seek it out.

Laertes realizes his wound is deadly as it has been
dealt by the poisoned sword. He tells Hamlet of the plot
to destroy him and explains that the wound the prince
has been dealt, though minor, will be fatal.

LAERTES: It is here, Hamlet. Hamlet thou art slain.
  No medicine in the world can do thee good;
  In thee there is not half an hour's life.
  The treacherous instrument is in they hand,
  Unbated and envenom'd. The foul practice
  Hath turned itself on me. Lo, here I lie,
  Never to rise again. Thy mother's poison'd.
  I can no more. The king, the king's to blame.

HAMLET: The point envenom'd too! Then venom to thy
  work!

Hamlet gathers all his remaining strength and stabs
Claudius with the poisoned sword, then forces him to
drink the remainder of the poisoned wine. Hamlet takes
Laertes's hand to signify forgiveness, before speaking to
Horatio to ask that he report the story properly.

HAMLET: Horatio, I am dead,
  Thou livest. Report me and my cause aright.

Fortinbras's army and the ambassadors from England then arrive on the scene. Hamlet nods, strangely content.

HAMLET: O I die, Horatio
The potent poison quite o'ercrows my spirit.
I cannot live to hear the news from England,
But I do prophecy th'election lights
On Fortinbras...the rest is silence.

HORATIO: Now cracks a noble heart. Good night sweet
prince,
And flights of angels sing thee to thy rest.

Fortinbras and the ambassadors are appalled by the sight of the four dead bodies. Horatio approaches the Norwegian prince and requests that he take charge.

Horatio: ...give order that these bodies
High on a stage be placed on view,
And let me speak to the yet unknowing world
How these things came about.

Fortinbras agrees and issues the required commands.

FORTINBRAS: Let four captains
Bear Hamlet, like a soldier, to the stage;
For he was likely, had he been put on,
To have prov'd most royal; and for his passage,

The soldiers' music, and the rites of war,
Speak loudly for him.
Take up the bodies. Such a sight as this
Becomes the field, but here shows much amiss.
Go, bid the soldiers shoot.

GLOSSARY

askant: slanting over

beteem: allow

cataplasm: plaster

chop-fallen: down in the mouth (unhappy)

mortal coil: life's troubles

conceit: concept, idea

crants: wreaths

crownet: wreath

discourse: power of reasoning

fardels: burdens

fretted: ingeniously decorated

gaingiving: misgiving

hent: opportunity

husbandry: savings

lauds: hymns of praise

lazar: leper

mountebank: peddler

ordnance: artillery, cannonballs

pendent: hanging

quicksilver: mercury

quietus: settlement of a debt

quintessence: essential nature

repair: go

rub: obstacle

slander: abuse

tetter: disease

unbated: (of a sword),unblunted, unbuttoned

unction: ointment

union: perfectly shaped pearl

vailed: lowered